Raising Goats for Beginners

A Hand Book to Raise Healthy and Happy Herd for Milk and Meat Production Plus Breeding, Routine Care, Marketing and More

By

Zelene Ward

Copyright © 2021 – Zelene Ward

All rights reserved

No part of this publication may be reproduced, distributed, or transmitted in any form or by any means, including photocopying, recording, or other electronic or mechanical methods, without the prior written permission of the publisher, except in the case of brief quotations embodied in reviews and certain other non-commercial uses permitted by copyright law.

Disclaimer

This publication is designed to provide competent and reliable information regarding the subject matter covered. However, the views expressed in this publication are those of the author alone, and should not be taken as expert instruction or professional advice. The reader is responsible for his or her own actions.

The author hereby disclaims any responsibility or liability whatsoever that is incurred from the use or application of the contents of this publication by the purchaser or reader. The purchaser or reader is hereby responsible for his or her own actions.

Table of Contents

Introduction 8

Chapter 1 10

Basics to Raising Goats 10

    Dairy Goats Vs. Meat Goats 11

    Pros and Cons of Raising Goat 12

    Goat Terms To Be Familiar With 14

    Popular Goat Breeds 16

    Choosing The Right Goat Breed 26

Chapter 2 30

Buying Goats 30

    Basic Questions 32

    Inspection 32

    Choose a Breed 32

    Health Status 33

    Registration 34

- Vaccination and Worming Schedules 34
- Nutrition 35
- Gender 35
- Gestation 35
- Milk Production 36
- Kids 36
- Mating 36
- Quarantine 37

Chapter 3 38

Farm Management 38

- Housing Your Goat 38
  - Shelter 38
  - Fencing 40
  - Bedding 41
- Protecting Your Goats from Predators 43
- Cleaning Your Goat Shelter 45
  - Keeping Your Goats Stalls Tidy 46
  - Select the Right Bedding Material 46
  - Stall Freshener 47
  - Quantity of Goats Poop in a Day 51

- Goat Mortality Management 53
  - Burial 54
  - Incineration 55
  - Composting 55
- Chapter 4 57
- Feeding Your Goats 57
  - What to Feed Goats 57
  - Goat Foods for Health and Weight Gain 65
  - What Not To Feed Goats 66
  - Rules of Goat Feeding 67
- Chapter 5 69
- Making Babies 69
  - Goat Breeding 69
    - Identification of Breed 69
    - Age 70
    - Preparation 70
    - Select a Compatible Buck 70
    - Breeding Type 71
    - Breeding Season 71
    - Gestation 71
  - Goat Kidding 71

Raising Goat Kids 73
    Care and Management of Newborns 74
    Castration 76
    Identification of Goats 79
    Disbudding and Dehorning 81
    Weaning 88

Chapter 6 90

Producing Goat Milk 90

  Goat Milk Cycle 90

  Training a Goat for Milking 91

  Milking Goat Milk 92

    Milking By Hand 92
    Milking With a Machine 97
  Storing Goat Milk 100

Chapter 7 101

Goat Handling and Behavior 101

Chapter 8 109

Harvesting and Marketing Meat Goat 109

  What Is Goat Meat Called? 109

  How to Harvest Your Goat Meat 111

 Markets for Goat Meat 117

  Knowing The Market... 118
  Marketing Channels 121
  Market Likes and Dislikes 121
Chapter 9 125

Keeping Your Goats Healthy 125

 How To Care For Your Goats.. 125

  Exercise 125
  Deworming 125
  Vaccination... 126
  Bloating... 126
  Grooming 126
 Have a Safe Environment For Your Goats 127

Conclusion 128

References 130

Introduction

Goats are witty, smart, intelligent, interesting, yet restless and stubborn. One minute, it can be exciting and another minute tiring.

Regardless of your purpose of buying goats and raising them, you have to be well equipped and prepared for the task ahead.

There's so much to learn about these unique animals and it's important that you dig deep and find the right information that will help you raise happy and healthy goats.

You must be fully aware that all areas of their lives are important and interwoven. Their environment, nutrition, health, breeding, milking, and other areas must be handled and managed in the right way, using the basic principles that apply to them.

The success attained by a goat producer is proportional to the knowledge he/she has acquired about everything that involves goat production.

Just as there's so much to learn from the habits and lifestyle of these interesting animals, there's also so much to learn about raising them.

In the pages of this book, you will find the simple principles that you need to raise goats on a small or large scale production.

You will be enlightened afresh and you'll understand that goat production is not gruesome if you know the right thing to do.

If in the past you have failed completely as a goat producer or you are a novice, that is just setting out to be a goat producer or you have a thriving Goat production enterprise, then this book is for you.

It covers all that is goat-related and will provide answers to questions or doubts that must have lingered for a moment in your mind.

Now, onto chapter one…

Chapter 1

Basics to Raising Goats

Everyone has their narrative. Raising Goats can be exciting, and for some schools of thought, it can be tiresome.

Regardless of your purpose of raising goats – commercial, personal, or just for fun, you must be well informed about the rudiments and basic information about raising these interesting animals. Then, your narrative can be a good and exciting one.

First, you need to know which type of Goat is best for you to raise. Of course, your interest and certain pointers will go a long way as factors that will affect your choice.

Are you interested in milk or meat produce?

Do you want a cute goat endowed with a charming personality or the boss goat with a domineering countenance?

If you can't handle the rough and bossy personality, then you should embrace the option of raising dairy goats. But, if you are interested in pushy and fleshy goats, you can opt for meat goats.

Let's find out the interesting features of these Goats.

Dairy Goats Vs. Meat Goats

Dairy Goats (Milk Goats)

You find them in various colors- white, gray, brown, and black. All shades of cute and, friendly animals. They are not domineering as compared to the meat goats.

It's a thrilling experience to be around them. They are playful. It's an accepted fact that they are good nurturers because they were bottle-fed by their owners, they are gentle and better with younger children.

The best part however is that you will never run out of milk if you choose to raise one. Not only do you have enough milk at your disposal, but you can also make goat cheese from it.

The downside is that it requires more work and time than meat goats

Meat Goats

You find them in a combination of two colors white and red. These Goats are quite muscular than dairy Goats.

They live to be butchered. You cannot get milk from them, but lots of meat. It's economical to raise them because they are not bottle-fed, but rather they drink their mother's milk.

Goat meat can be pushy, they like to head-butt and may occasionally push you down and chew your clothes. Nevertheless, it doesn't require so much time, effort in raising one.

Now that you must have decided on the type of goat you'd like to raise. It's paramount that you must know the pros and cons of raising goats.

Pros and Cons of Raising Goat

Let's start with the pros.

1. Goats Are Charming.

Baby goats are super cute. And, with the diversity in colors and breeds, that you find amongst goats, they are no doubts one of the cutest animals around.

2. Easy Milking Process.

Yes. It's easy to get milk out of a goat. While it's true that they don't produce so much milk like a cow. However, because of their small size, it's easy to handle them.

3. Less Space.

These creatures are browsers and small in stature, hence the need for a large space is not necessary when you want to raise them.

4. Financial Gains.

You can make more money by raising goats because they make lots of babies easily. You can generate income by selling them

The Cons of raising goats include:

1. Health Issues.

Goats are prone to all kinds of parasitic infections. This huge challenge can pose a big risk to their general well-being.

2. They Are Destructive.

Goats destroy everything. Everything in their sight. They can equally be messy.

3. They Are Noisy And Loud.

They love attention. Love to be everywhere and heard. And not to forget the bleating.

Goat Terms To Be Familiar With

You should be familiar with certain goat terms to help you navigate through their world.

1. Billy Goat: This is an intact (uncastrated) male goat. It also a male older duck

2. Brush Goats: They are simply unknown breeds.

3. Caprine: This is the technical term for goat. It comes from the Latin word – caprinus.

4. Chevon: This is the French word for goat

5. Nanny Goat: This is the opposite of billy goat. It is an older female goat, that must have given birth.

6. Bleat: This is the sound a goat makes.

7. Poll: This is the point between the ears of a goat.

8. Polled: This is a goat that is born without horns.

9. Bucks: They are male goats, that are prepared for breeding.

10. Doe: They are female goats that are ready for breeding.

11. Wether: This is a castrated male goat.

12. King and Queen: King is the male buck in the herd and queen is the main alpha female in the herd.

Popular Goat Breeds

Goats come in several breeds. Each breed has its peculiarities. Below are the few popular breeds of goats.

Alpine

Alpines are big goats. They also come in medium size. If you are particular about the size of your goats or want to enjoy a rich production of milk. Alpines are the perfect fit. And the features are amazing.

Tall ears.

Long and pointed nose.

Weight of about 135 pounds and good height.

Big teats, that you make the milking process easy.

Alpines are good friends that tag along with you everywhere you go.

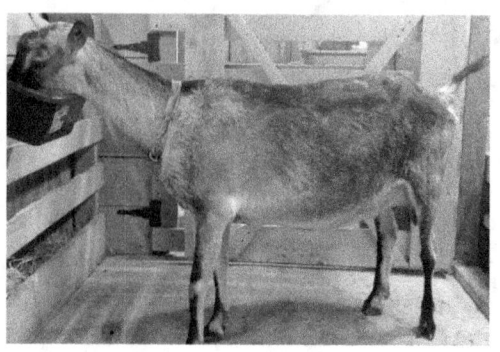

Boer

A Boer is reserved especially for meat production. Their weight increases spontaneously faster than other breeds. This short and stalky goat has high resistance to infectious disease and thrives in hot dry climates.

They are white colored animals with brown heads, long cute pendulous ears, and a short face.

Kiko

Kiko goats share a lot of similarities with the Boer goats. You can get milk from them but just like the Boar goats, they produce less milk than the dairy breeds

They have striking features- straight noses, medium length ears.

Primarily, they come in white colors and other variety of colors

They are healthier because they are usually worm-resistant.

In general, Kiko goats can be an additional meat goat that you need

Lamancha

Cheesy is the word that best describes this breed of goats. They have tiny ears that look like they don't have ears at all.

Cool, calm, and rich in milk production.

They thrive in diverse weather conditions. Lamanchas enjoy human interaction, thus making them a good company.

Nigerian Dwarf Goat

They have a small size and a friendly nature that makes them alluring. Everyone, especially children love this particular breed of goats. Because of their small size, you do not require a large space to raise them. They have small teets, which can make the milking process tiresome for those with arthritis and carpal tunnel syndrome.

Nubian

Often referred to as a dual-purpose breed of goat. Nubians are goats with large sizes, long pendulum ears and a lovely Roman nose.

As compared to other breeds of goats, they thrive well in hot weather and have a longer duration of the breeding season.

Because of their big sizes, they need more space than goats of sampler sizes. It's a known fact that overcrowding is detrimental to all animals, especially goats. Therefore, you just ensure that you have adequate space before getting a Nubian Goat.

Their milk has a unique and lovely flavor as a result of the high butterfat content of about 5% or possibly more.

A Nubian Doe is usually 30 inches tall, while the bucks are about 35 inches. The expected weight is within 135-175 pounds and for the bucks, about 200 pounds.

It's an interesting fact to know that Nubians are very friendly goats, easy to handle and work with. They enjoy interacting with humans. They are known for their long teets which makes the milking process easy and enjoyable.

They are generally lousy and enjoy making noise. They yell at the slightest given opportunity.

As a result of this big size, it's acceptable that they are well suited for families with young children.

They are a perfect fit and addition to your family.

Oberhasli

They have striking features – beautiful coats and stunning colors. They are warm around people and friendly. They do not get frightened like other goats. Also, known as an amazing family milk goat. They are often used as pack animals, simply because they enjoy working and thrive well in grooms.

You can get about 1½ gallons of milk from them daily because they are great.

Does are usually about 28" tall and bucks about 34" tall. Their weight also differs with Does weighing about 120Ibs and bucks 150 Ibs.

Generally, some breeds of these goats do not thrive in a wet climate, this is why you must ask adequate questions before buying to be sure they can live in your climate.

They are very hardworking dairy goats with small size, making them ideal for growing families that reside in a dry climate condition.

Saanen

If you have spotted a goat with an all-white color, that's definitely a Saanen.

They are endowed with short straight ears and a unique face that makes them stand out in a herd.

They produce milk in high quality and volume.

A big diary goat that is unapologetically friendly. Most breeders love this breed of goats because they are gentle, this making them a good addition to young families with young children.

Does weigh about 145Ibs and Bucks about 200Ibs. Does are 31" tall and bucks are 35" tall. Although they have a low buyer fat content, they thrive well in any climate. They also have high resistance to diseases.

They earned the name gentle giants of the goat world because of their large size.

Toggenburg

This is the oldest dairy goat. They are good milk producers, and their milk has low butter fat. Majority of them have battles (appendages on the throat). This is one of their striking and irresistible features.

They have so many color variations. They can be gray, tan, amongst others. They have a striking resemblance with the Alpine sporting beards in both genders- bucks and does.

They are medium-sized animals with does weighing 125 Ibs and bucks 200 Ibs. Does has a height of about 30" and bucks 36".

They are affectionate and gentle animals. They are also very sensitive and alert. They thrive in cold weather and are exceptionally well at motherhood.

A Toggenburg goat is probably the oldest known dairy goat that is a great milk producer.

Although this list may not cover all, nevertheless these are the most common types of goats in the world.

You should consider your location, family size and age before you buy a goat. Ensure that you do a thorough check, this is necessary for you to get the best breed for your family and environment.

A healthy and fit goat will bring you so much joy and less stress. You should also ensure that you have the right living conditions for them- forage, good housing, feed, and water.

You get to enjoy a lot of benefits from raising these animals if they are well-groomed. Perks of fresh milk, cheese and butter, amongst others are what you stand to enjoy.

Choosing The Right Goat Breed

Choosing the appropriate and ideal goat breed for your family or farm can turn out to one of the best or worse decisions ever made in your life. It's always exciting to get the next available goat in the market, however doing thorough research is of great importance.

You need to know your purpose in getting or raising a goat. Is it for the meat, fiber, diary, as a pet, sales of kids, as pack bags, or as companions to bigger animals?

Choosing the right goat breed for your farm or homestead can make or break your experience with goats. It can be exciting to rush to buy the first goat you find, but taking your time and doing a bit of research will really pay off in the long run.

When you conclude on your reasons for buying and raising a goat, then you should put the space into consideration.

Space

If your farm is large, with adequate space and expansive pastures, then you can comfortably raise any goat breed of your choice.

Typically, goats are herd animals, you must ensure that you have at least two to prevent them from developing depression or food aversion in an extreme case.

Also, you must ensure that you will be able to provide optimal security that they need.

Goats are stubborn, persistent, with dogged determination. They are intelligent at running away, therefore if you will be raising goats, you should install heavy-duty fencing. Some small-sized goat breeds like Nigerian Dwarf or Pygmy can be catered for in a small area.

Big-sized goats like Alpine, Boer, Saanen, and Nubian will florish in a large environment. You must be aware that bored and restricted goat, turn out destructive and uncontrollable.

Temperament

Just like humans, goat equally has their own personality traits. For instance, Nubians are loud and strong-willed. They are uncontrollable and difficult to manage. You need to be patient and loving towards them. The moment you establish rank amongst the goats, they can be faithful, and kind animals.

Small goats are fun to be around, because of their playful nature. Their small size enables them to be rambunctious without being destructive.

The bigger diary breeds are tagged the gentle giants. Alpines are sweet and not difficult to please. The fiber goats are really different, they are the most docile of all the animals

They are slow, calm and a delight to raise. They experience bullying when they are raised with other dominant breeds. You need to watch out and be vigilant.

If you want to learn more about the personality of a breed, you should spend adequate time with them. A breeder might be able to help you with more information.

Attend shows or auctions and enquire about the temperament of the herd from the breeder.

Check goat forums and learn about the breed you have developed an interest in.

Expenses

The cost of buying a goat is not expensive. Goats are sold everywhere within the ranges of $50-$1000, depending on the lineage and size of the goat.

Ideally, a good goat will be about $200.

It's also advisable for those looking for goats as pets for themselves or their family to check their local animal shelter. It's common to find great animals that need a home and shelter for free.

The expenses of raising goats are from feed and housing. This is hugely dependent on size. Small-sized goats require small space, less feed and smaller pasture.

Goats that are raised primarily for meat or dairy will need more feed compared to those raised as pets. It's advisable that you do adequate research on the feeding plan for your goats and compare the prices. Alfalfa or grass hay or source grain. The choice is yours to make.

Regardless of the choice you make, goats are easy to raise. You learn a lot in the process. Take time to do your research, be strategic in your planning and you will find the goat that is the perfect fit for you.

Chapter 2

Buying Goats

It's no doubt that your goat shopping moments can be exciting. Goats are affordable, however, you should make the best choice when buying a goat.

Unhealthy animals can spread infectious diseases amongst your herd. Thus spiking up your veterinarian bills. One important factor you must not ignore when you are planning on breeding a new goat is the said animal's gene because it will become the crucial part of their genetic configuration forever.

I'm sure you desire to raise healthy and fit animals in your herd.

You will find lots of breeders online. Ensure that you conduct thorough research about the person you intend to purchase a goat from. Usually, breeders have a functioning webpage. Check the website thoroughly and read the details about their farm. Look into their history and the reviews of prospective customers.

If you are not satisfied with the information you got on the website, call them or send an email to them. A good breeder should be available to answer your questions. It's important they share the pictures of the goats with you.

If a breeder is not forthcoming with the response that you need, please don't patronize the breeder. It could be a loss on your own part in the long run.

As soon as you get to the farm, scrutinize the animal's living condition. Is it hygienic? Does the animal have access to basic amenities – clean water, good housing conditions, etc.?

Check the goat's herd mates. Are they healthy? Do they have shiny, soft coats? Do they have bright eyes? Are there signs of injury or infection – limping, wounds, shivering, isolating themselves from other animals, and balding patches? Is the barn tidy, and void of ammonia odor?

Let's check out some important checks you must perform before buying a goat

Basic Questions

There are basic questions to ask in order to provide you with the information that you need to aid the buying process. You should enquire about the basic details of the goat- age, breed, weight, sex, and size.

Inspection

You must meticulously look at the goat from head to toe.

Does the goat have a soft and shiny coat? Check if her hooves are in good shape.

Does the goat have a bright eye?

What's the personality? Curious, friendly or wild?

Check the body for signs of injury – wounds, lumps, swellings, tenderness, and hair loss.

Choose a Breed

It's recommended to go to different breeders and taste the milk of different breeds, in order to know what you like.

Every breed has its specific taste of milk and strengths, which is always a factor that will influence your decision. This will enable you to meet different goat breeds to know the temperament you like. And essentially, you can see diverse goat keeper's operations and do the relevant comparison to provide great ideas about the appropriate practices. This also helps you connect with other goat keepers, so you can always have someone to respond to your questions.

Health Status

You must know the health history and status of any animal you are buying because ensuring that your herd is disease-free is paramount. Find out from the breeder if they have records of herd testing for the year, and if they didn't have it. Ask if they don't mind a blood test to be run on the animal.

You may have to shoulder the financial responsibility if the breeder isn't responsive because it is a rewarding investment for the future of your herd.

The vital tests that your animal must undergo before joining the herd

- Caprine Arthritis and Encephalitis (CAE)
- Tuberculosis(TB,)

- Caseous Lymphoma (CL)
- Johne's Disease Brucellosis

Registration

Registered goats are more valuable than unregistered goats, even if they share a lot of similarities in terms of breed and quality. With a registered goat, a traceable lineage is guaranteed. Also, it provides the opportunity for them to participate in milk production programs and shows.

Finally, it enables the offspring to be duly registered too.

Vaccination and Worming Schedules

Every goat keeper has their vaccination and worming schedule. There have been controversies on what is suitable for the animal, but it's advisable to do your research on available goat vaccines and chose which is important, instead of joining in the baseless debate.

You must know the vaccines/wormers the animal has taken that year, to prevent a double dose.

Nutrition

When you want to buy an animal, you must know what they currently feed on. It can be stressful for a goat to experience abrupt changes in its diet.

It's best you continue with the feed the goat is accustomed to, and you slowly change the goat to a new feeding pattern

Gender

If you will be buying does, male or kid, there are differences in most areas, so you should ask certain questions relating to each gender.

Does: Generally, they are the most valuable goats to purchase. A high quality for does can fetch you more money. If she is bred, you just ask about the duck. And if he's a resident, you should endeavor to see him.

Gestation

What is breeding like for her? How many kids does she give birth to? It's common for goats to give birth to twins, and triplets as a second outcome, followed by a single birth. You should desire to have an idea of what to anticipate regarding the number of goat kids you can sell or have as an addition to your herd.

Milk Production

What's the quantity of milk she produces daily? Remember that having a high producing milk doe makes the kids valuable. You will be raising high-bred quality goats in the long run.

When is she milked?

It's possible that the breeder's milk schedule may not fit into yours. The good news is that the doe can adjust gradually. Does are milked 12 hourly, however you can try adjusting her milking time gradually by 15 minutes daily until you have found what's convenient for you.

Kids

When and where were they born? When they were weaned? Did they receive treatments for Coccidiosis? Make inquiries about their parents and ask to see them.

Mating

How successful has the male goats been with mating?

What is his personality type and temperament? , especially in a rut?

Most males experience personality changes when in a rut, you must ensure to know if they can be controlled or managed.

Quarantine

It's important that all new goats must be quarantined for about 1-2 weeks. They should be wormed in a different and separate farm and allowed to dispel parasites they have taken in from a previous farm before you allow the goat to join your herd.

Chapter 3

Farm Management

Housing Your Goat

Regardless of your purpose of raising goats- commercial, fun, or other reasons, goats need protection from elements that include rain, snow, heat, and wind, among many others. They are wanderers and are always in the habit of getting out of enclosures, thus making security a vital issue for these animals.

You will need to provide solid and tight fencing for them.

Shelter

A basic goat shelter doesn't need to be glamorous or over the top. With a hoop house, you can provide maximum shelter for goats.

Windbreaks, or trees, a pole barn, or a three-sided shed with a roof is ideal for your goats during the grazing season. Keeping them out of the drafts is the most important thing.

You will require more than the basics if you are kidding in the winter. You will need a strong building for your pregnant and/or lactating does and kids. You can make use of livestock panels to separate the space into different pens for individual groups of does and kids.

As you create and arrange the goat house, you should put into consideration where you will keep feed, straw, bedding and basic goat-related equipment. You must ensure that you leave enough space for waterers and feeders, to help keep things tidy and minimize wastage of feed.

For your goats to be able to have access to woods, pasture and other areas, you must create close to 15 Square feet per goat indoors as a sleeping space. Otherwise, you may need close to 20 Square feet per goat for sleeping space and 30 Square feet for exercise.

And adult goats require at least a four-foot-by-five-foot kidding pen. Therefore, you should put into huge consideration this space as you create your goat shelter, depending on the quantity of does you will breed per time.

It's possible to have different does kid at various times in the same pen, if you constantly clean and sanitize the pen between kidding.

Fencing

Fencing provides safety for your goat and other possessions. It must be secure, not only to keep the goats in but also to keep predators- bears, dogs, coyotes, foxes and others out.

You should use perimeter fencing around the whole goat area or property border, and cross-fencing in the goat area to prevent overcrowding and ensure the goats are separated from one another. Fencing can be permanent or temporary.

Temporary Fencing

Temporary fencing aims to separate the bucks from does and weaned kids from does.

It may be poly tape or wire, high-tensile electric wire, or electric netting.

For high-tensile wire, you should get 5 to 7 strands of wire spaced about 6 inches apart on the bottom and a little more for the wires on top (8 to 10 inches)

Permanent Fencing

The construction can also be of high-tensile wire. However, if you want to prevent the smaller predators like foxes from getting in, then this is the best bet.

Because they crawl easily under a six-inch high wire, woven wire fencing is the best bet for perimeter fencing. In order to keep the predators out and goats in, you should install a strand of barbed or electric wire at the top.

Bedding

If only people knew the importance of bedding for a healthy goat, then it will be considered as a topmost priority. It has a lot of benefits which include ensuring the goats are warm, protecting them from draughts and providing a good and comfortable material to lie on.

The bedding should be totally mucked out frequently. This is basically the removal of all bedding. The whole living area must be washed and cleaned with bleach during this time.

You will need some materials which include: sand, wood pellets, straw, bark, dried leaves, chopped corn cons, oat hulls, shredded paper without ink, corn driver (stalks and husks). Using each of these materials has its benefits and downsides. Most importantly, it depends on what is readily available in your vicinity and the associated costs. And, the materials must be of high quality, because goats often eat some of the beddings.

You must ensure the bedding is dry as possible. Wet bedding mold and often becomes a source of respiratory disorders. In addition, it will no longer serve the purpose of keeping the goats warm.

Below are four tips to help keep the beddings dry.

1. Ensure that the goat's drinking water is kept outside, to prevent it from spilling on the bedding.
2. Ensure that the beddings are on top of the pallets, such that all droppings will be on it and keep the beddings clean and intact.
3. If there are wet areas and droppings on the beddings. Ensure that you remove them and put

fresh bedding. This is a good way to keep the bedding longer.
4. An affordable and excellent option for bedding is a bottom layer of sand that will help to absorb the urine and a top, thick layer of straw.

Protecting Your Goats from Predators

One of the overwhelming challenges encountered by most livestock producers is the lingering issue of predation. This is a make concern for goat, poultry and sheep producers. It is also true that cattle and horse producers can equally experience losses caused by predation.

The leading predators for sheep and goats are usually coyotes and dogs, while predators like bobcats, foxes and birds of prey may persist as a problem in certain areas. The predators that give people a sleepless night are dogs and coyotes. Generally, coyotes do well in all places and usually cause problems irrespective of their location. Nevertheless, producers in the cities experience greater losses to domestic dogs. Also, feral dogs can cause problems in certain areas.

When you are planning to shield livestock from predators, the primary thing you should do is to review the laws guiding predator control and livestock loss.

Every state has laws and guidelines that help producers manage and control predators on their respective farms. All States have an individual way of handling the situation. There's usually a difference in requirements and enforcement of proof in each state. You should check local news before starting any control program.

Nonetheless, there are three major ways of predator control or a blend of these methods that have been result-oriented such as guard animals, special fencing and lethal methods of control.

All these methods have their benefits and downsides. However, they work appropriately when combined. A lot of goat producers can attest to the fact that when you use a guard animal along with good fencing, it will be potent enough to control losses.

The use of lethal control will be needed in unique cases. However, it must be used with caution. Because this method involves poisons, hunting and trapping. Usually, the state places some restrictions on lethal control; you should reach out to game and wildlife officials or law enforcement before opting for this option.

Finally, according to some producers, a combination of good fencing with night pens, plus lethal controls is more effective.

Take a survey and seek the right counsel to ensure that you implement a solution that is perfect for your farm and location. Also, you mustn't go against the law when using any lethal method of control.

Do a thorough check before you start.

Cleaning Your Goat Shelter

One way to help your animals stay healthy is by keeping your livestock and their shelters clean. When your animals are on a farm, you must have encountered challenges as you try to clean their waste. The hardest part is cleaning goat poop. This is why some goat keepers ensure their goats have diapers to reduce the stress of cleaning up after each defecation.

You must not be discouraged by the messy details or allow it to prevent you from ensuring that your goats stay neat. You must know how to keep goat stalls clean, and the tools you will need for the task.

Keeping Your Goats Stalls Tidy

It's a sight sore to see goat poop littering a goat stall. Not only is it difficult to clean, it also makes the unhealthy.

You must understand that goats love to poop and pee constantly. Therefore, they will always have a shelter that's not entirely clean. They are messy animals and sometimes litter the stall floor with hay prior to eating part of it. This is essentially why you must create and maintain a good cleaning system. The following tips will help you maintain a clean environment in your goat stalls.

Select the Right Bedding Material

You must be right on track in this area. Picking the right and most appropriate bedding for the stall is the first part to create the clean environment that you desire. You should use Pine and Straw bedding for the bedding material.

Usually, pine bedding is made from little pieces of pine trees. It is very absorbent, thus making it effective in ensuring that the stall is odorless and clean.

The downside to using this is that the moment it becomes dry, it suddenly turns sticky and messy.

Straw bedding is always still intact when dry, it doesn't become messy. It's affordable than pine bedding and you can clean it easily with a pitchfork. The downside of using it is that it doesn't absorb the liquid that comes from the pee. Instead, the pee remains on the floor of the stall.

Stall Freshener

Because goats poop and pee often, it's expected that their stalls will always smell bad. The right choice of bedding can eliminate some odor, but it doesn't get rid of everything.

A stall freshener helps to keep the environment tidy and air clean. Therefore, it is a must-have. There are several types of stall fresheners. However, the most effective are powdered.

Directions

Pour freshener on the stall floor or specific areas that goats tend to pee in.

Mode of Action

Generally, the ammonia released from goat pee is dangerous to their lungs. The goats shouldn't stay or live in the exact spot. What stall fresheners do is absorb ammonia, thus leaving the environment healthier and safe for the goats. Lime water is also a good choice. When you use it to wash in the stalls, it eliminates dangerous bacteria and keeps everywhere clean.

Litter Systems

There are two types of litter systems for goat stalls. You should choose the one that suits your goat stall.

Deep Litter System

This is the first litter system. It is used during the cold weather months. For this system, you have to provide the animals with a compost floor.

Directions

1. The first thing you should do is to start bleaching the stall.
2. Rinse thoroughly and allow the floor to dry.

3. Spread a large quantity of stall freshener on the floor.
4. Cover with a pine bedding layer or straw.

With this type of system, you don't have to clean the stall again. You just need to cover with fresh beddings the moment you see the stall is getting too dirty.

Non-Deep Litter System

Non-Deep Litter System is ideal for those that clean frequently. It also works for warm weather. For this system, you need to scoop the bedding every two weeks and use a broom to clean out the stall.

Directions

1. Tidy up the environment by cleaning the stall and ensuring the floor is dry.
2. Spread stall freshener on the floor.
3. Open a new bedding and spread the cover on the entire stall
4. At regular intervals, sweep the soiled beddings.
5. Clean the stall and ensure the floor is dry.

6. Always replace the bedding with a new one when the need arises.

One point worth noting is that goats are carefree about where they pee or poop. You should make it a point of duty to always check the areas outside the stall and keep it clean and tidy as needed.

Frequency of Cleaning

The number of times you clean your goat stall varies, depending on the type of litter system you are implementing.

If you will be using a deep litter system, you don't have to clean the stall frequently, because you will be putting a new layer of bedding to cover any waste. You should always replace the bedding when the need arises.

As for the non-deep litter system, you have to clean the goat stall often. Possibly, after one or two weeks. When you clean the pen often, it helps the goats stay healthy.

Quantity of Goats Poop in a Day

Goats tend to poop at intervals of each feeding period. However, when they are sick or when there are abrupt changes in their feeding, they poop more often.

Also, the quantity of poop from goats that eat hay is quite different from that of goats that graze.

Typically, goat poop is slightly bigger than a raisin. The size varies from a hand full to a 1- foot pile. The size of the poop is influenced by various factors -goat's size and diet.

5 Basic Tips for Cleaning Goat Poop
Cleaning up after goats is sometimes tiring, but it can be a good experience if you know what to do and how to do it. Most goat owners waste so much time cleaning and rearranging the bedding. It is important that the environment must be tidy to prevent the goats from developing worms. It's easier to clean goat poop when you use beddings that don't absorb too much. As a result, most farmers prefer using straw bedding, because of the wide space that allows poop and urine to sift down the floor. The area of the straw that is soiled can be covered with another fresh layer of straw.

You will need the following tools to clean goat poop- shovels, brooms, rakes and wheelbarrows. It's advisable to use a pitchfork if you use straw bedding. With a leaf blower, you can easily push the poop and bedding out, to reduce cleaning frequency.

There are various methods used for cleaning goat poop. The following tips are effective and yield the desired results.

1. With a layer of straw and sawdust, you can soak up the pee and poop, instead of using straw bedding.
2. Shift through the straw with a leaf rake. Flip and drag it with a wide bow rake. Then, pack it into a bucket with a shovel.
3. Push the bedding and poop aside with a leaf blower. Pack it into a wheelbarrow with a shovel.
4. With a pitchfork, pick up the bedding and sweep the leftover poop with a broom.
5. Pick the poop with an extra-large dog poop scooper.

As tiring and awful as it may be, you must clean goat poops for your goats to stay healthy. The good thing is that several methods make it less demanding. Choose the method that is convenient for you and one that works for your goats.

Goat Mortality Management

Generally, in a normal meat operation, about 10% of the kids born live do not make it before the weaning period.

So, what is considered normal? A death loss of about 5% in the breeding herd.

Biological and environmental Safe methods of dead animal disposal must be implemented, for various reasons – to serve as a form of protection for the health of herds and farm personnel, prevent soil, waste and air contamination, and avert problems with agricultural and non-agricultural neighbors.

According to a sound health program, it's recommended that goats that died from unknown causes, must be transported to a Department of Agriculture Diagnostic Laboratory for an autopsy to be conducted. Therefore, the burden of carcass disposal becomes the responsibility of the state.

The producers will have to pay for the autopsy and next carcass disposal by incineration.

For certain reasons, some dead goats will be disposed of by the farmer. The methods of disposal of carcasses are burial, incineration, and composting.

Burial

This is the most popular and affordable method of dead animal disposal. For this disposal method, a pit is usually dug and the carcasses will be placed in it.

Generally, deep burial is often recommended (4-8 feet).

It is not recommended to cover dead animals with lime, because it retards decomposition. You shouldn't bury dead goats in places that leaching occurs.

The downside of this method of this goat disposal method is the odor and easy accessibility of scavengers to pits that are not well covered.

It also increases the possibility of ground and surface water contamination, which the producers will have to be responsible for.

Incineration

This method totally destroys carcasses and pathogens.

There are limitations to the capacity of many incinerators, therefore this method of disposal is best for goats that weigh less than 50 pounds.

Generally, it's expensive to buy and operate an incinerator. For instance, it may cost about $2,500 to buy an incinerator with 600- pound capacity and $1,000 to maintain it. Some specific incinerators cause air pollution and produce objectionable odors.

Composting

The mode of action of thermophilic, aerobic bacteria converts nitrogen-rich (for example dead animals) and carboniferous (for example straw and sawdust) materials into bacterial biomass, compost and humic acids.

The byproducts generated during the composting process are carbon- dioxide, air and water. This product is nutrient-rich and is often used as fertilizer because they are free from harmful pathogens.

In the poultry and swine industries, composting is widely used for getting rid of dead animals.

Typically, carcasses are put in a bin that contains sawdust. This creates a perfect environment for the growth of bacteria. The appropriate carbon to nitrogen ratio for bacteria is usually about 30:1.

The action of the bacteria heats the compost piles to a high temperature of about 160°F. In few weeks, the carcasses are less, with only brittle bones left that can easily crumble. When you turn the compost pile by simply moving it to a secondary bin (new bin), after 2 weeks, it boosts more decomposition and helps in maintaining high temperature, thereby promoting further decomposition.

Chapter 4

Feeding Your Goats

What to Feed Goats

Majority have the misconception that goats eat everything. This is very untrue because goats do not eat everything, because they cannot digest everything. And, certain foods are poisonous while others have nutritional value.

The following are foods that you should feed your goats with the right nutritional value for them.

Chaffhaye

Basically, this is grass or hay. You will start by cutting them into small chunks and layer with molasses. Afterward, you put it in a bag, to patch it inside the containers. It mixes good bacteria into the hay and makes it easy for the goats to digest.

Pasture & Browsing

They have high nutritional value. It helps in the digestion process.

Good pastures include Bahiagrass, millet, Sudan grass, and millet, a mixture of grain grass and clover, and sorghum.

Pasture can be used in place of hay.

Browsing aids the pasture process in the grazing season. It's healthy for goats and shields them away from contagious diseases.

Garden and Kitchen Scrap

This is time-saving and affordable. They have a high nutritional value. Examples of scrap include banana peels, orange peels, tomato ends, and garlic skin.

Dried fruits, fruits and veggies can serve the same purpose.

Sweet foods are not usually recommended for goats because they make goats overly dependent on junk products.

Hay

Goats can eat hay. It's affordable and contains a rich quantity of protein and nutrition. If on your farm the pasture feeding system is great, then you can feed your goats with hay, when the grazing is not available.

They can also enjoy it on cold or rainy days.

Examples of good hays are soybean, clover, lespedeza, vetch and alfalfa.

Vitamins and Minerals

Goats need Calcium, Phosphorus and salt because they contain minerals that are needed for the goat's health. They also need Vitamin A, D and E. Baking soda is a source of vitamins that relives the goat of bloating.

Black seed, sunflower seeds are a source of vitamin E which helps milk enrichment and development of reproductive systems and muscles. Kelp meal is a good source of iodine, which helps in boosting milk production. They also need Probios, for the good functioning of the rumen.

Grains

If you are not able to get the necessary foods for the goats, you can make up with 12-16% of grains.

Regardless of the goat species, grain is an important food item.

They must eat grain every day.

Mature goats must eat 30%-40% grain foods in their feed.

Grains contain protein and carbon, making it very important for goats. Grains can be whole, textured, pelleted, and rolled.

Cereal grains include rye, oats, barley and moil.

Baby goats cannot digest grains well.

Feeders and Waterers

Feeders

As a goat owner, you need different types of feeders to feed the goats. You can make cheap homemade goat feeders from home-used, inexpensive or recycled materials. Goats can sometimes be destructive, this is why you need to ensure that feeders are durable and strong.

The materials you need for making feeders depend on the type of feeder. Goats basically require hay, grain and mineral feeders. You will need the following materials to make homemade goat feeders- nails, PVC pipes of different widths, various pieces of dimensional lumber and plywood, chain, and different types of wooden pallets.

The tools include saws, tape measure, hammers and drills.

Let's take a look at some feeders

Trough Feeder

This is the most appropriate feeder for serving grain or goat pellets. It provides a wide trough that the goats need.

You need about 4-inch diameter PCV to make it. Cut the PCV to the trough length that you desire. Divide the PCV length in half, and design two half-moon pieces. Put one piece of 2-inch treated limbs at an end of the trough. Follow and trace the shape of the curve to the wood.

Afterward, split the 2 pieces of wood to this shape in order to create the end caps of the trough. Put the wood pieces inside the PVC and ensure that you secure it with wood screws. You can see an eyebolt to the top of each wood. Then, attach a chain to hang the trough.

Hay Feeder

Hay feeders need openings. Ensure that the openings are small to prevent the goats from getting their head stuck but wide enough for the goats to have access to the hay. Use 2-by-4 board pieces to make hay feeders for some goats.

Put the boards closely together and create a crate with spaced slates.

Loose Mineral Feeder

Your goats need supplements alongside their diet. For this, they need free-fed loose minerals with their regular foods. PVC pipes are ideal for this purpose.

To make a loose mineral feeder with a PVC pipe, you should get a female adapter, a male threaded cap, 4 inch PVC Pipe along with one 45 -degree elbow connector, and an end cap.

To seal the feeder, you should use a PVC primer and cement. Put the primer at the top opening in the 45-degree elbow connector and to the end of the PVC pipe.

Let the primer sit for some minutes, then, push the pipe directly into the connector, when you have applied the thin layer of cement to the two ends. Now, you will have a long pipe that has an opening of an elbow connector.

Repeat this process with the other end of the connector and female adapter. To close the bottom, screw the male cap in.

Let the feeder sit for 24 hours before you proceed. To hang the feeder, drill holes in the PVC and fasten a chain or rope to it.

You may also want to drill the feeder directly to the walls in the goat shelter. When you have succeeded in creating the feeder, fill in with loose minerals at the top, and use the end cap to seal it up.

Waterers

Goats should be able to get enough water for their stage of production, age and weather conditions. The most effective method of providing water to goats especially those in paddocks or yards is Automatic Waterers. If it's not readily available, then adequately sized containers should be available to ensure the right quality and quantity is available for age, body weight, number, and type of stock, weather conditions (available shelter, humidity and air temperature), production level and dry matter content of the feed provided.

Generally, goats need 4-5 liters of water daily and 10 liters during lactation. Recently weaned kids and lactating must have access to water. The water supply should be clean because the goats might refuse to drink it if it's dirty or contaminated.

Automatic water floats should be protected to prevent the goats from damaging them.

How Much Do I Feed?

How much to feed your goats is influenced by lots of factors – size, level of physical activity and age. Also, the purpose of raising goats – for milk, cheese or fun will also influence your decision.

You should always remember that the changes to the type and quantity of food must be gradual. Abrupt changes to diet can lead to digestive issues and stomach discomfort.

It's best to introduce new foods gradually.

Averagely, goats require about 2 to 4 pounds of hay daily. The particular figure depends on the amount they forage on pasture. The more they forage, the lesser the hay. The less the forage, the more the hay.

Ensure that you feed grains to your goats with caution. Adults only require 1½ pound a day. Kids need less, about ½ cup is enough.

Goat Foods for Health and Weight Gain

Goat owners experience all kinds of challenges while raising their goats. An ill or poor weight gaining is a corner to the owner. Goats need high protein compared to other livestock. Generally, a normal diet should be made up of 7% of portions. However, milking goats require about 14% of portions. The goat needs a balanced diet plan to have good health and maintain the right weight.

You must provide clean water. And, you may decide to add minerals in tiny portions of minerals.

This food list will help your goats gain health and weight.

Black Sunflower seeds which is rich in selenium and vitamin E.

Minerals (1-2%).

Grain (7- 10%).

Pasture (80-90%).

What Not To Feed Goats

Goats shouldn't eat unhygienic food that could cause further health issues. Ensure that they don't eat trash like cigarettes or papers alongside their food.

Dog or cat feeds should never be given to goats for consumption.

Also, the following should be excluded from their meals- Milkweed, Azaleas, and Wild cherries, Avocado, Crotalaria and Chocolate.

Plants with oxalates, for instance, Lilacs, Kale, Holly bushes, Rhubarb leaves, peach and palm leaves, and any nightshade vegetable

Finally, toxic plants to goats include Grass, Berries, Weeds, Cherries, Poison Ivy, Poppy, Lily and Ferns.

Rules of Goat Feeding

These are the rules that apply to goat feeding.

- The quantity of green feed, vitamins, minerals and feed must be in the right proportion and adequate.
- Supplements should be given to goats to boost their immune system, and milk production.
- Adequate attention should be given to improve the goat's body condition.
- Goat feeding shouldn't be contaminated with bacteria, parasites or germs.
- You can control their diet with hay.

A Short message from the Author:

Hey, I hope you are enjoying the book? I would love to hear your thoughts!

Many readers do not know how hard reviews are to come by and how much they help an author.

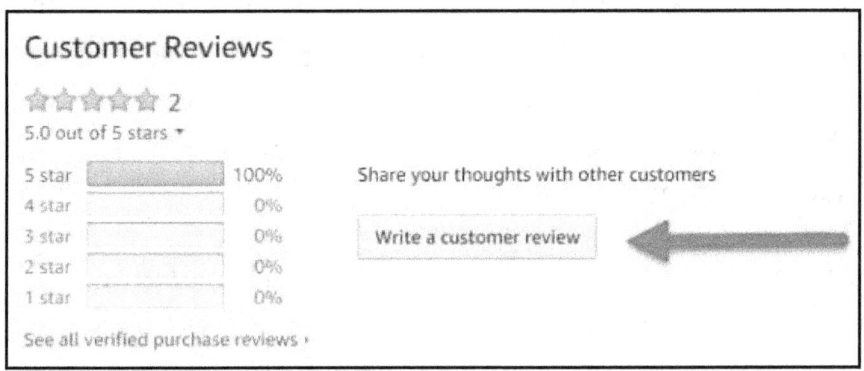

I would be incredibly grateful if you could take just 60 seconds to write a short review on Amazon, even if it is a few sentences!

>> Click here to leave a quick review

Thanks for the time taken to share your thoughts!

Chapter 5

Making Babies

Goat Breeding

Knowing about goat breeding helps in building and sustaining a successful goat farming business. It would help you to multiply the goat population and subsequently increase your profits if you are in the goat business for profit-making.

For most farmers, breeding can be challenging. The factors listed below will help and guide you in have a successful outcome in your goat breeding process.

Identification of Breed

Know the temperament and bloodline of your goat. It will help you know the type of breed you have and if the goat can be bred successfully. Depending on your type of goat, you will need to find a compatible buck for your does/doe.

You might need an expert in this area if you are filled with uncertainties.

Age

Ideally, a doe becomes mature and ready for breeding in a year. If you are looking out for quality, you shouldn't breed your does before their first birthday.

Also, keep the buck and doe away from each other, till they get to the right breeding age.

Preparation

The health of your goat affects their breeding process. The doe must be healthy to be considered fit for breeding.

You shouldn't breed a weak or ill doe. Ensure that they feed adequately on nutritious meals. Frequent checkups and deworming procedures are vital.

Select a Compatible Buck

Choose a compatible buck for the breeding process. You can talk to various goat breeders to find what is perfect for your does.

Breeding Type

You should decide on the method of fertilization you want to use, before entering your doe to her heat cycle. You can even use both natural and artificial breeding.

While natural breeding is more effective, artificial breeding is more expensive and not always successful.

Breeding Season

Fall is the usual breeding season of goats. In this season, a doe becomes heated several times, at almost an interval of 18-22 days between 2 heat cycles. It's best to start the breeding process in the early stages

Successful fertilization is dependent on timely mating.

Gestation

Gestation period is always about 5 months. The does must be well feed with nutritious and healthy food. You must take care of the does and incoming babies.

Goat Kidding

Kidding could take place on pasture, or you can make provision for does with a ventilated shelter that is both dry and clean. Pay close attention to the animals for any assistance they may need. For beddings, you can make use of pine or straw shavings. Within one – six weeks before kidding occurs, an enlarged udder will start developing in the pregnant animals. Other signs that kidding is getting close include either side of the tail of the doe being hallow, isolation of the doe from other herds and teats starting to get filled with milk.

Two weeks before kidding occurs, the doe's ligament muscles will start to soften and relax. If it is the doe's first time of kidding, these development signs may not be shown only after two weeks or more after kidding. Prior to labor, typically one to two days, the doe's teats will be enlarged and will be full of milk and will start to display signs of nervousness such as restlessness, pawing at the ground, and lying down. Toward the end of the labor (typically, the last 12 hours) the doe will display regular bleating sounds and the tail will be either straightened out or elevated slightly.

Normal delivery most times take about five hours.

When the water sac breaks, the doe will give birth in about 30 minutes to one hour. If the doe encounters difficulty by pushing so hard for more than 30 minutes without the appearance of a water sac or kid, then you need to help the doe yourself or get a veterinarian for support. Goats typically give birth to three kids but could be more in rare cases. This process will be repeated with each kid.

As soon as the kid is birthed, do not allow the cord to break naturally, however, if the sac remains unbroken, it should be broken for the doe. Also, wipe off any mucus from the nose, mouth, and throat of the newborn kid.

If it appears the kid is not breathing, rubbing the kid so hard using a towel will help to stimulate its respiration. Also, when you place a straw up the kid's nose, this will stimulate the kid to sneeze, thus helping to clear the airways. As soon as the doe has kidded, ensure her placenta is shed. If the placenta goes undetached after 12 to 18 hours, reach out to your veterinarian.

A few hours after been born, normal kids will try to stand, looking to nurse its mother's udder. So, ensure that the kid receives the first milk (colostrum) from its mother after birth (the first one - four hours is recommended).

Raising Goat Kids

A newborn is fragile and needs attention, care and love. You must ensure that you have the capacity to raise a goat kid to avoid problems that could arise or lead to the death of the newborn.

Care and Management of Newborns

1. Ensure that newborns are breathing. Discard materials from their mouth and nose. Use a clean towel or rag to clean and dry the newborn. With a piece of straw gently inserted into the nasal page, you can stimulate breathing in a weak one.

2. Keep them warm and most importantly, dry. Ensure the bedding is soft, dry and clean. And when it's wet, add extra beddings or change it. In a pen, a heating lamp can adequately increase the temperature.

3. Cut the umbilical to a length of 1.5 inches and spray with a tincture of 7% iodine, to prevent infection.

4. Don't separate the kids from does, except Caprine Arthritis Encephalitis (CAE)- positive does or bottle rearing kids. The bond between the mother and kids must be adequately developed.

5. Guide and assist newborns to stand up and suckle. They need the colostrum after birth for their health.

6. If suckling is hindered or does is not producing adequately, you can bottle feed colostrum to kids. If kids are too weak to stand up, they can be bottle-fed or tined. Give approximately to their appetite. The leftover colostrum should be refrigerated and warmed (38-39°C) when they need to be fed. The bottle must be cleaned before and after feeding. Colostrum should start half an hour after the kids are born and repeated close to 5 times daily. Ensure you oversee them and don't force them to drink.

7. Diseases can be transmitted through colostrum and milk. Diseases like Johne's disease, Caseous Lyhadenitis, and Brucellosis and, Caprine Arthritis Encephalitis are dangerous. Therefore, if a doe is infected with any of these diseases, kids should be separated from their mother and not given colostrum and milk.

8. Ensure that the environment is well ventilated, clean and safe form predators.

Castration

Male goats grow very quickly. They become fertile around seven weeks. It's important that they are castrated early in life.

There are various ways of castration. You must choose what is best and comfortable for your goats.

Banding

This is a popular type of castration. It's easy and not so scary. Goats can be castrated from 8 -12 weeks of age. You should never castrate them before 4 weeks or after 4 months. Banding involves these processes.

    A. Antitoxin.

You should administer one CC of tetanus antitoxin, to prevent tetanus and its complications.

    B. Gather Your Materials.

You need an elastrator and castrator ring for the castration of your goats. Keep the rings in the refrigerator, to ensure they don't deteriorate in warm conditions. They retain their shapes if they are properly stored after purchase.

Five minutes to the procedure, dip the rings in rubbing alcohol for about 5 minutes. For proper sterilization, place the rings on the elastrator. On the elastrator, you will find prongs at the end of it that will hold them in place.

C. Positioning.

When you are ready and the materials are in place, place the goat kid in the right position. You need two people to do this. One will be holding the goat and the other person will be controlling the elastrator.

The person holding the goat kid can place the head on their lap, with their hindquarters directed towards controlling the elastrator.

D. Fix The Ring.

When the kid is positioned correctly, open the ring by squeezing the handles of the elastrator. The individual operating it should place the ring over the testicles and scrotum. You must ensure that it gets around both testicles and below it before you think of removing it from the elastrator. Don't squeeze the elastrator further, gently remove the prongs from the band.

Be sure that both testicles are below the castration ring and no shifting has taken place before you remove the elastrator.

   E. Watchful Waiting.

The blood flow to the testicles will be cut off and they will gradually dry up. In about two weeks, the banded parts will fall off.

In cases where there are loose skin still attached, use a sharp, clean scalpel to slice and remove it

Surgically Castrating Goats

This is a more intense procedure than banding, if you are inexperienced, you should go to a veterinarian to castrate your first goat. They will teach you all you need to learn about this process.

For this process, someone should hold the goat with their hindquarters pointed to you. Slice the scrotum open with a sharp and clean scalpel. The testicles will be out completely and if they are still hanging to their spermatic cord, slice further to release it. They will fall to the ground. Avoid stitching the scrotum closed to prevent invasion of infection. Rather, introduce antiseptic to the wound to allow it to drain and tp prevent infection.

This is the most effective method of preventing infection.

Emasculation

This is a safe and less risky method of castration, probably because it's faster or no blood is involved.

You will need a castration plier or burdizzo. You should use the size meant for sheep or goats.

With the goat in the right position, Slide the pliers where the spermatic cord is located (between the body and testicles). Press down on the pliers to crush the spermatic cord. This action will make the goat let out a high-pitched sound. In 15 minutes, the goat should be back to its normal state, as the procedure is over.

Identification of Goats

Animal identification is essential. It allows the producer to maintain good records for the smooth running of his farm. There are 2 major types of identification: Permanent and Non-permanent.

Permanent are ear notches or microchips and tattooing, and Non-permanent are tags, paints and chalks.

Ear Notching.

This is often employed as a common way of identifying goats. It is very visible from a distance, and allows identification without the need of catching the animal. It can accommodate numbers to 9999.

Tattooing.

It is permanent, if done the right way. It's basically making a needle-like projection in the goat's skin. It's best to sterilize the equipment and clean the goat's ears to avoid the spread of certain blood – borne diseases.

Ear Tags.

You can use this to identify individual goats in the herd. Because they can easily break or rip out of the goat's ear, most producers use two ear tags. Before using the ear tag on the goat, you must record the ear tag number that is assigned to the goat. The tag must be inserted between the cartilage ribs on the ear.

Microchip.

This involves the insertion of a microchip in the tail web or base of the ear of the animal. The microchip must be thoroughly scanned after insertion to be sure it's reading correctly.

Disbudding and Dehorning

Disbudding is the removal of buds and thorns. Dehorning involves removing horns from older goats. You simply stop the horn from growing when you disbud.

Horns can pose a lot of hazards, like getting injured or death to other goats or their owners. You can disbud from 4-10 days of life.

You need a sharp knife, goat disbudding iron, heavy-duty gloves, homemade animal healing salve, helper and goat disbudding holding box.

Steps To Disbudding & Dehorning

STEP 1) Make use of hair clippers to trim the hair around the little buds on the head of the goat. Then, plug in the dehorning iron & preheat for about 10 minutes.

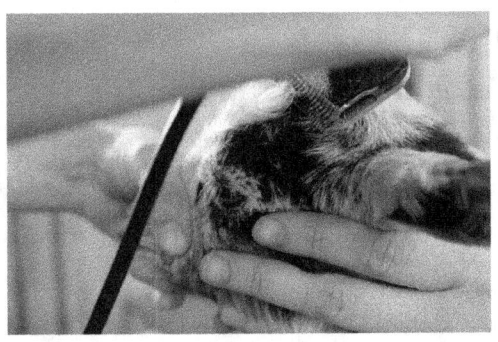

STEP 2) Put the baby goat in the disbudding holding box. You will need a **disbudding holding box. It is very important!** Baby goats are strong and you will need help to hold them. To avoid getting too stressed, you should get someone (a helper) to hold the goat.

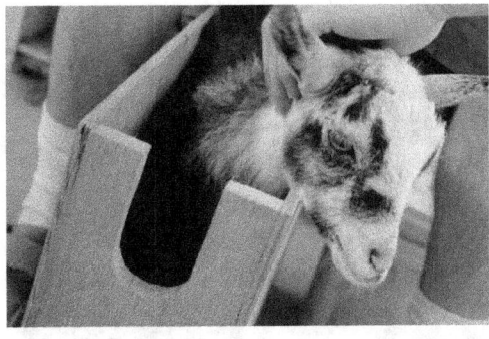

STEP 3) Check to see if the goat is rightly positioned by the helper. The head must be through the u-

shaped slot, with the board on top with the helper sitting and the head pulled out while the helper holds the head with the ears folded backward. Before you start, ensure that you test the iron on a piece of wood. It's ready if it burns nicely in two seconds.

STEP 4) Place the hot iron down around the little bud of the goat. The open circle goes around the tip of the bud. Let the weight of the iron be your pressure. You will slowly rotate the pressure around in a clock-wise manner, for 3-4 seconds. For males, burn for 5 seconds. The helper can blow on the smoke so the disbudder can see what they're doing. You should see a copper ring in the base of the bud.

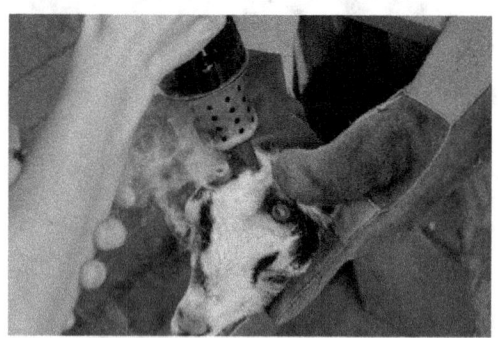

STEP 5) That's it. The nice copper ring. If you don't get it the first time, try again.

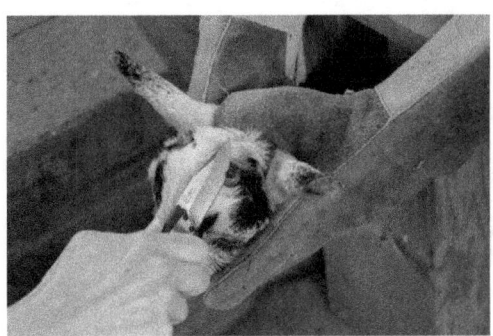

STEP 6) Then cut off the bud with a knife. Ensure that you do it from the base of the bud. It comes out easily.

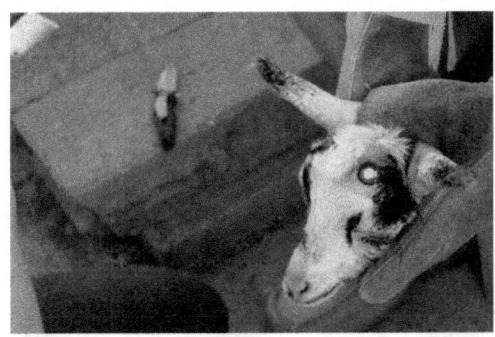

STEP 7) The base of the bud may likely bleed or not. If there's a bleed, there's absolutely nothing to worry about.

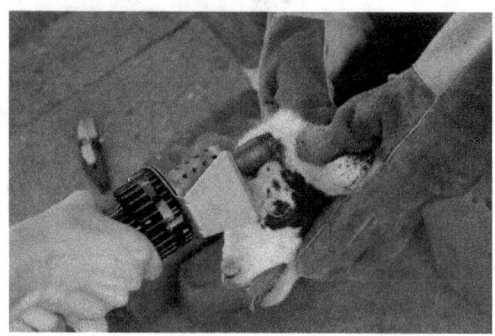

STEP 8) Burn the base of the bud using the side of the iron. Move the iron around to ensure you get a good burn.

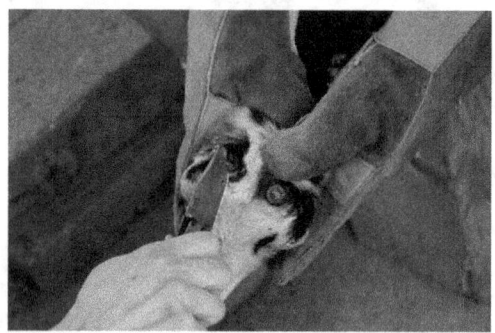

STEP 9) Repeat the same process on the other side to cut the bud.

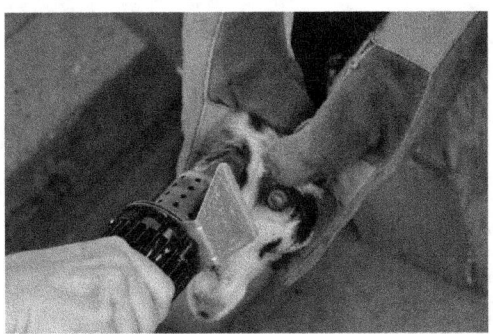

STEP 10) Using the horn, cauterize and seal the top.

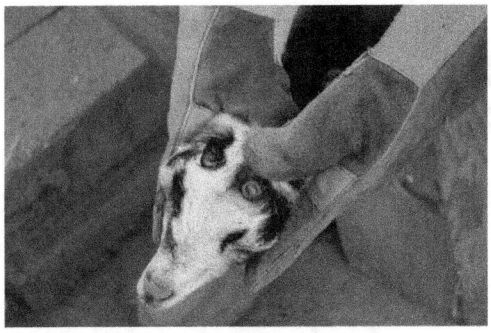

STEP 11) You should go again at the base of each ring for at least 3 seconds.

STEP 12) Check the burned buds to be sure you didn't miss any spots. If everything is fine, allow the mother to bottle feed or baby back with its mother for comfort.

STEP 13) Let the burned buds rest. Avoid applying anything on it the first day. You can add a healing salve the next day. Don't fret if you notice small oozing and some drops of blood. However, if the bleeding is severe, you want to cauterize it once more. It is always not necessary though.

In the next two weeks, the hair will grow back and you won't see any horns again.

Note that you will need an additional step if you have a male baby goat.

This is because male goats have extra growth hormones in their bodies, and you may have to burn an extra ring overlapping the original ring.

Burn another ring for 4 seconds, directly behind the original ring. This will prevent scurs from springing out and decrease the scent. This is one major step you must never skip with male goats.

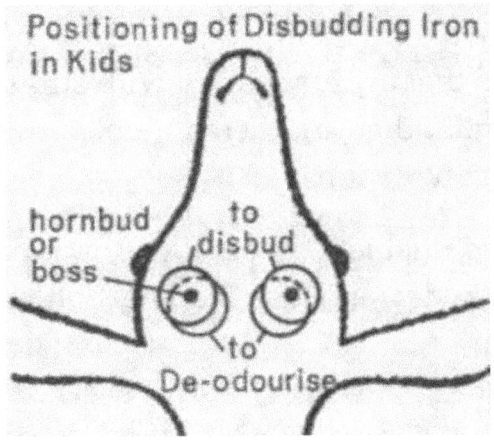

Weaning

As soon as a kid is born, does start nursing. From a week to 10 days, the kids can eat grasses, hay or leaves. Goats are known ruminants. Some sections of their stomach are not mature in the first week to 10 days of life. Therefore, they need to depend on their mother's milk.

Weaning takes close to three months. The kids should be left with their mother for a natural weaning process. It's best to wean kids when they weigh 2.5 than their birth weight.

You should apply caution about feeding the kids after weaning dairy goats. Usually, the kids are separated from the mothers. The does are producing milk.

After birth, separate them from their mothers and keep them in areas that are embedded with straw. Afterward, you should milk their mothers for colostrum, because it is essential for newborns.

If the kids are unable to get colostrum, mix commercial colostrum powder and use feeding bottles or tubes to feed the kids.

Chapter 6

Producing Goat Milk

Goat Milk Cycle

Typically, goats have reflexes that hold back milk for their kids, as they nurse. She will abruptly stop the milk flow when she notices that the rest of her stores need to be kept for the babies.

The kids must be weaned at 8 weeks old. The freshening stage of her milk commences the moment the kids no longer need the milk from their mother.

A nanny goat must not be milked if she hasn't entered the 'freshening' portion of her milk cycle. At this stage, the nanny goat has entered her milk cycle and doesn't need to save milk for her kids. This stage lasts about 12 months.

The 'going dry' stage of the milk cycle is when to breed her again.

Generally, a goat's milk dries up 2 months before she can be rebred.

Training a Goat for Milking

Some goats do well at milking than their counterparts. Most first-timers don't like to enter a milk stand or remain there, compared to an experienced nanny.

It's as if you just wrestled with a bear when new nanny goats have their milking sessions. Nevertheless, you shouldn't be discouraged, because the transition and expected behavior get better and in a short while, the nanny starts to know what is expected of her.

Goat Milk Training Tips and Hints

1. They need a distraction, a delicious one will be perfect. Give them some grains or their favorite snacks as they are being milked. Ensure the other goats are kept away, to avoid the nanny been aggressive.
2. Address and treat the goat calmly as you lead her to the milking stand, till you finish.
3. You should put one of your hands on the goat's rear legs, if she fusses on the milking stand, to prevent kicking the bucket of milk.

4. Some farmers use goat hobbles to keep the nanny goat calm in the milking stand. You can try this method
5. Use a small bucket when milking a small stature dairy goat.

Milking Goat Milk

Milking By Hand

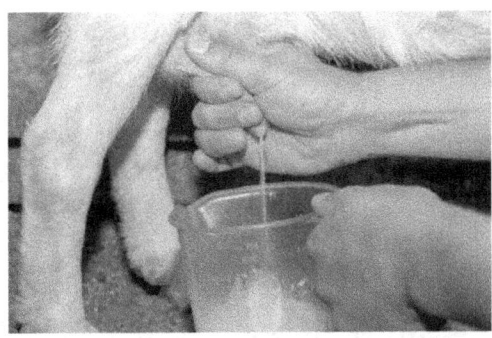

Goat's hand milking is not so easy. As a farmer, you will need the right facilities, time, and adequate knowledge of breeding and how to manage breeding does, good hygiene, and endurance. If you are not sure about certain things, you shouldn't hesitate to talk to an experienced dairy goat farmer.

Procedure

You must always wash and dry your hands properly before you start. You should equally clean the udder, with a medicated teat wipe or disinfectant, and then wipe dry with a clean cloth or paper towel.

And to avoid water droplets from drooping into the milk and chapped teats, you should dry your hands and the udder properly. Because goats don't like cold hands, you should warm your hands first.

Hold the base of the teat with your thumb and index finger. Don't attempt to grasp the udder. Hold the milk in the teat canal and prevent it from returning to the udder by closing your thumb and index finger.

Subsequently, close the second finger, third and little finger to propel the milk out into the bucket. Throw away the first squirt or two as the milk may not be hygienic. When you feel tired with one hand, make use of your other hand.

	DON'T milk like this; it destroys both teats and udder attachment to the body.
	Because milk can run out of the teat into the bucket or back into the udder; you must close your thumb and first finger
	Afterward, close your second finger, to make the milk squirt out.
	Now, close the third finger. Avoid jerking or pulling down. Make use of steady pressure.
	Proceed to close your little finger and then, squeeze with your whole hand

	This time, you should release the teat and let it fill up with milk. Repeat the process with the other hand.
	When the milk flow is coming to an end, nudge the udder to see if the doe has let down all her milk.

Routine

If trained properly with care, dairy goats adapt quickly to being milked. It's best for young does to get accustomed to milking shed, even before they ever get pregnant. Occasionally, they can be given some feed in the milking stand. When it's time for them to be milked, it will be a hassle-free process.

"Share milking"

Regardless of your plan to milk the does, you must ensure that the kids have their first milk- colostrum for the early days of lactation. It is good for newborns.

Generally, kids need milk. An adult doe with good health and well-fed can still raise at least one kid and at the same time provide for her family.

To share milk, you need to reduce the access of the kids to the doe, so that the doe can be milked. The doe can be milked in the morning and the kids can be with them in the afternoon till evening when they will be separated.

Facilities

The milking stand can be installed in a section of the shed. It must be a raised platform, plus a restraining crate, and a head bail for holding her. The equipment must be cleaned and disinfected after milking with an antiseptic.

Drying off

There are various methods of drying off. You can reduce the quantity of milk you extract at each session or you milk out completely at each session. The latter method reduces the chance of mastitis. They are prone to developing mastitis if the milking stops because bacteria are liable to invade the teat canal.

Nafpenzal, which is a dry goat treatment is administered after the last milking if the udder is totally milked out so that the absorption into the udder is good.

Milking With a Machine

Milking with a machine can be easy with the following steps:

STEP 1

To start, you must wash your hands. Fill two buckets with water. One with warm rinse water and the other with warm water mixed with a half cup of bleach. Take them to the milking area for cleaning the machine when the process is over.

STEP 2

Put the milk bucket close to the stanchion, and position properly the silicone gasket in the milk bucket lid. Put the milk bucket cover on the bucket and pull with a force the clamp directly over the cover to clamp them together.

STEP 3

Test the milking setup to be sure it's working well. Put the claw valve lever below the claw in the 'up' position on the inflations and switch on the pump to ensure it's functioning properly. Ideally, the vacuum gauge should read about 10 – 12" and the inflations should start suctioning in a few seconds. Everything must work before you start milking.

STEP 4

Place the goat on the stanchion and give her some grain, this serves as a distraction while she's being milked and makes the experience fun for her. That way, she will look forward to being milked each time.

STEP 5

Use udder wipes to clean her udder. Then, express milk from both teats into a strip cup to be sure there's no problem with the milk. Be sure there's no lump, blood, or anything strange.

STEP 6

Start the milking process by starting the pump and inserting the teats into the inflation. Milk will come through the inflations in 4 minutes. If the milk is no longer flowing, break suction on the teats and gently remove the inflation.

STEP 7

Clean the teats once again. Spray with FightBac. This serves as a form of protection because it prevents bacteria and mastitis.

You should equally weigh the bucket to know the quantity of milk she produced.

Take the goat back to the stall.

STEP 8

The process is over. You can disassemble the milking machine.

Once everyone's been milked, remove the lid from the milk bucket, place it on top of the rinse buckets, and take the milk bucket inside.

STEP 9

Empty milk with a funnel lined with milk filter into sterilized glass jars. Cover and refrigerate the milk.

STEP 10

Rinse the machine with warm water and then with bleach water and dry.

Don't forget to clean the milking area.

Storing Goat Milk

1. Because milk can easily get harden and stick to your milk bucket, you should invest in a seamless stainless steel bucket. Keep things tidy and clean, by rinsing out with cool water, after each milking session. Afterward, use hot water or natural cleaner to rinse.
2. Filter the milk immediately.
3. Keep the milk refrigerated at 35-38 degrees.
4. Store your milk with glass jars.

Chapter 7

Goat Handling and Behavior

As a goat owner, you must know how to handle the animals you raise.

Below are general ways to handle goats effectively.

- You should not pull, lift or catch a goat by its head, fiber, tail, legs, or ears.
- You should handle the heavily pregnant with care and keep them off stressful situations.
- You should perform general husbandry with your goats standing.
- You should never transport injured or sick animals, except for veterinary treatment. Even at that, it's best for the veterinarian to visit.
- Don't upend goats onto their rumps.
- You should never isolate your goats. They are herd animals and like to be around other goats. If the need arises to isolate a goat, give them the opportunity to see other goats.
- Goats should be trained to approach and follow a bucket of food when you call them. When they

respond, you should reward them by giving them access to a treat or the bucket. However, you should give treats sparingly.

Goat Behavior

Goats exhibit different behaviors depending on their age, sex and mood.

Kids

Bottle Raised Kids

Kids pick habits from their mothers, other kids and adults in the herd.

Bottle-fed kids don't quickly learn how to eat grain, hay or browse, compared to herd-raised kids.

They also struggle with learning how to drink water quickly.

They don't eat other foods unless you withdraw the bottle from them

Getting Missing

At this age, they get missing often. They like to hide in caves or holes. It's a perfect idea to put bright colored collars on them to be able to find them easily.

Chewing

All goats including kid goats explore their world with their mouths. Because they have no hands, they use their mouth to explore as they chew.

Climbing

Baby goats love to climb. It's fun for these young animals.

Sneezing

Goats use sneeze sound to wade off impending danger. Did you know that goats use the sneeze sound as an alarm? They use a sneeze to warn each other of danger (be it real or imagined). Young goats sneeze as part of their play. If you watch your goats you will begin to notice their use of the sneeze sound.

Head Butting and Head Pushing

Head Pushing and Butting is playful for kids goats. And they cannot get enough of it.

Adults - Both Male & Female

Violence & Herd Order

Goats are violent, no matter how adorable and sweet they may be around you. On some occasions, they will get violent with each other. This a natural occurrence amongst them

Petting

They love to be petted. They enjoy it when you scratch their front chest and underarms.

Head Butting and Head Pushing

Older goats love to head butt, but they fight more. They do so to establish dominance.

Adult Females (Sometimes Wethers)

Fighting

Goats determine their place amongst the herds by fighting. Fighting is a characteristic behavior of goats, it is in their nature. So, simply allow them to fight when it occurs. Immediately a winner is determined and their place is validated amongst the herd, they will no longer fight again.

Smell

Bucks develop smell but does and wethers do not. Keeping your bucks that smell in the sample place with your does (not advisable) will rub off on the does. Milking the does will also get the smell in their milk.

Dominance

One thing about goat herd is that they are hierarchical, so much so that does have a place in the herd. A doe can display dominance over another doe by;

- Ramming or hitting
- Forcing her to rise from her resting place
- Flapping the tongue
- Pawing their leg and,
- Blubbering

Heat

Does exhibit some characteristics that are "bucky" when in heat. Others that are not in heat can likewise display these characteristics toward does in heat. They do this by;

- Flapping the tongue
- Pawing their leg and,
- Blubbering

Adult Males

Courting/Mating

Bucks get the ladies into the mating mood by displaying some mannerisms such as peeing, which is more often than not, displayed toward does in heat. Giving that breeding and the exercise of dominance are very related, you will notice that does, wethers, and bucks show dominance over themselves (or even to you) by displaying some traits. These displays are very normals. A buck that is in the mood does not mind the sex he wants to mate. I must say that a buck may attempt to mount on you if he displays these traits, this means he is crushing on you. Some example of the traits can be;

- Flapping the tongue: The buck lowers his head and tongue flaps at the does side (or you).
- Pawing their leg: With its leg straightened, the buck paws at the does side, which is most times

performed simultaneously alongside tongue flapping.
- **Blubbering:** Usually performed toward the doe (or you) and could be done together with tongue flapping and pawing of the leg.

Urinating

When bucks become matured and goes into rut, which is the male equivalence of heat (in the Fall), they will begin to pee on their faces and front legs. With some kind of "attachment spray" on their penis, they can literally spray their urine inside their mouth. Eventually, he becomes coated with urine (which does finds irresistible by the way) on his face, beard and legs. As the rut ends (in the Winter) he may cease or may not cease to pee on himself.

Aggression

Bucks become very aggressive as they mature. There is no exception because the calmest and loveliest of bucks can still confront you, likewise his companions, (usually in the breeding season). Bucks that are aggressive to humans isn't a good thing and need to be trained to understand that you are dominant to him.

Mother Goats

Pawing

New mothers paw at their new kids and not with the intention to attack them; this is to get up and moving. Pawing does not mean a mother is refusing her kid, and if she refuses her kid, she will show this by ignoring her kid or simply use her head to butt at it so that her kid can leave her alone.

Chapter 8

Harvesting and Marketing Meat Goat

Goat production involves harvesting and marketing meat goats. This is simply butchering a goat and cutting the parts.

What Is Goat Meat Called?

Goat meat also known as chevon or mutton is gotten from mature animals. In certain parts of the world, it is also called cabrito or capretto, which simply means kids or young milk-fed goats.

These are the 5 best meat goats.

1. Boer Goats.

They mature quickly than other breeds and have a good fertility rate and outcome. Mature female Boer weighs 200 pounds and the Billy goat weighs 340 pounds.

2. Spanish Goats.

It is a known breed amongst small farmers and homesteaders that reside in hot climate. Previously, they were not only meat producers, but for raised for other purposes – mohair, hide processing and diary. They weigh about 50-200 pounds.

3. Kiko Goats.

Mature female Kiko goats weigh 110 pounds, while mature male Kiko goats weigh 176 pounds.

4. Myotonic Goats – Tennessee Goats

They are referred to as the land care breed of livestock. Kidding and milk production comes natural to this breed of goats. They are resistant to parasites and weigh 200 pounds the moment they reach maturity.

5. Pygmy Goats

They are muscular and their meat has a nice flavor and is super tender. If you cross-bred with a Nigerian Dwarf, you'll have a dairy goat and purpose meat.

How to Harvest Your Goat Meat

STEP 1: Cut the throat; ensure that you cut through both jugular veins, so that it bleeds well.

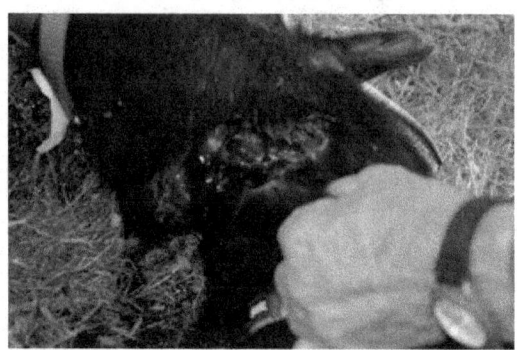

STEP 2: Cut the skin starting from ankle to anus on one of the back legs and then cut the skin up the belly to the neck. Start to skin the goat by separating the skin from the meat.

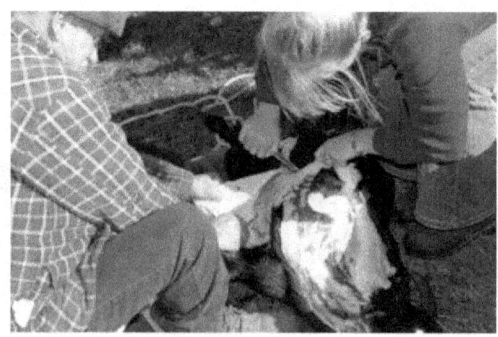

STEP 3: The moment the skin is off the front of the body, make two incisions with your knife, between the tendon and the bone. These holes are used for slipping a rope through so that you can easily hang the goat. Make sure that the goat is hanged high enough for the work to be comfortable.

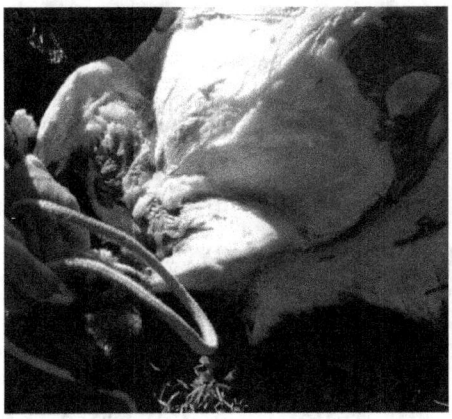

STEP 4: When you finish skinning the goat completely, you can cut the head off.

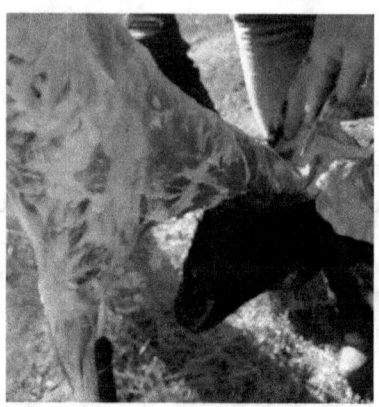

STEP 5: Carefully cut the belly open, do not cut the intestines. Just cut through the skin and the moment you reach the breast bone, you will need to use a meat saw to finish cutting to the level of the neck.

STEP 6: Start letting the contents fall out. Use the meat saw and cut through the pelvis. Hold the rectum with one hand and slit the anus away from the inside of the goat. Avoid cutting the intestine or rectum. Allow the contents spill out of the cavity.

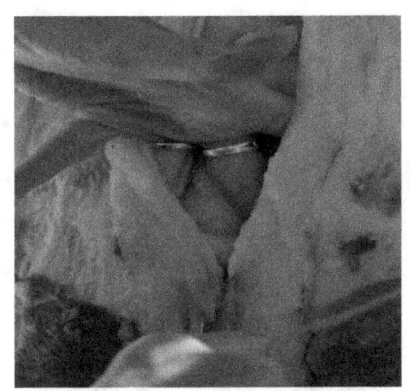

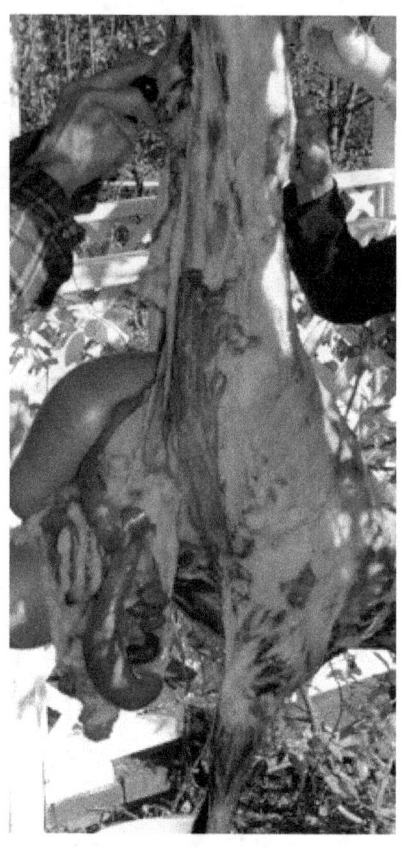

STEP 7: Set aside the heart and liver. Cut the heart and let it bleed. Wash the heart and liver properly and then put them in cold water until you can put them in a refrigerator.

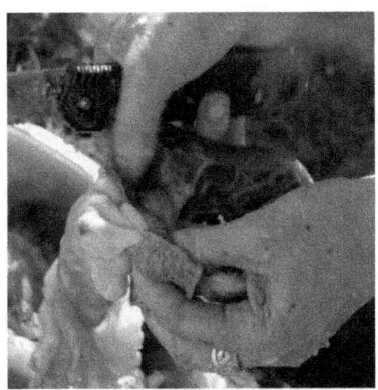

STEP 8: Cut away from the throat and neck area the esophagus and trachea.

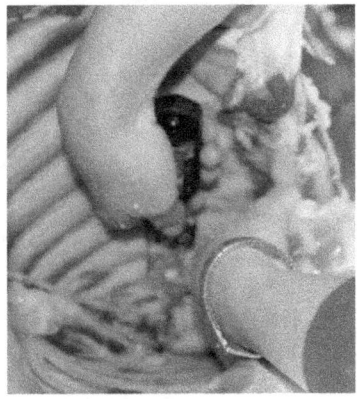

STEP 9: Using a meat saw, cut the carcass in two equal parts from tail to tip. You now have two sides of goat ready.

Markets for Goat Meat

Goat meat has a unique flavor. It's tender and leaner than other red meats. Because of its tenderness, it's considered a meat with low fat. Cabrito are roasted meats of goat kids from age 4 – 8 weeks that are used for barbecue meat and loved by people from certain regions because of their tenderness. Chevron is basically meat from goats of 6-9 months.

Goat meat is widely loved and consumed all over the world, particularly in developed countries, it is the 4th most consumed meat in the United States.

Just like other meat production, it requires good husbandry, in certain areas like feed, sanitation, shelter, water and health.

Goat production has tremendously increased in the United States, in the last decade, as a result of the economic value. Factors like increased number of ethnic groups living in the country, major preference for goat meat and its products and drive for self-sufficiency have increased the growth of goat production in the country.

Knowing The Market

The starting point of knowing the market is to understand the rules guiding meal handling in most cultures. For Muslims, it's required that their meat must be 'Halal' or 'Lawful' to their holy book. This simply denotes that it must be slaughtered using zabiha methods.

Halal practices involve slaughtering with the use of zabiha methods, but if this method is not available, some Muslims will still take Kosher killed meats, and others may also take meats killed by Christians

When a Zabiha Kill is taking place, the animal faces Mecca and Takbir (which is basically a blessing that invokes the name of Allah) is declared as the animal is been killed.

Any goat that has eaten pork is considered unclean by Muslims. And a Kosher involves the animal been killed by a trained devoted orthodox Jew, with a well-sharpened knife with no bodyguard.

Slaughterhouses usually apply for a religious exemption to do Kosher and Halal slaughter. It is your obligation to ensure that your meat meets the requirement of your customer's standard of Kosher and Halal. Some cultures like Caribbean, Oriental and African like their carcasses to be singed or scalded as a major part of the process.

Goat Marketing Terms

Because of the growing market in the world for farm-fresh products, people prefer organic meats as much as other choose grass feed meat. The following are descriptions of these words.

"Organically certified" meats are from livestock that has been groomed in compliance with the National Organic Programs. Their production is usually certified by a private certifying agency or accredited state. Strict guidelines are laid down.

"Natural "can be described as a food label that doesn't denote how an animal was raised, but the way it was processed. They don't contain preservatives, coloring agents and artificial ingredients. So long the raw product remains intact, meat can be dried, smoked, roasted, or ground.

"Grass-fed" cannot be referred to as an official marketing claim. The USDA Agricultural Marketing Service (AMS) has over the years tried to come up with a standard for this said marketing claim. Therefore, AMS concluded that livestock whose primary energy source all through their lifecycle is made up of at least

80% forage, grass, green or range pasture can be referred to as grass-fed. Certain producer associations believe that this level should be as high as 95%.

"Humanely raised and handled" meat is from farms that have taken part in a private certification program, for instance, Humane Farm Animal Care (www.certifiedhumane.com), a consumer certification and labeling program that uses the standards designed by a scientific animal welfare committee.

Marketing Channels

There are various ways of marketing goat meat such as producing kids for commercial marketing firms, direct marketing off the farms, and supplying the meat to specific markets. Aside from these, there are specific markets for health-conscious clients that desire low-fat diets and restaurant trade for specific ethnic food that contains goat meat.

The success of this business depends on how well the producer pays attention to the major aspects of management, breeding, marketing and health.

Market Likes and Dislikes

Certain cultures have their preferences when buying live slaughter goats. For instance, immigrants from Korea like black or dark colored goats because of their religious or medicinal significance in their country, or they just prefer it.

Most buyers do not like Pigmy, Angora and white goats. But, a meaty goat doesn't come with all the restrictions. Currently, most markets have a high preference for goats with traces of Boer breeding. Goats that have good horn sets or flashy markings can generate more income.

The end... almost!

Hey! We've made it to the final chapter of this book, and I hope you've enjoyed it so far.

If you have not done so yet, I would be incredibly thankful if you could take just a minute to leave a quick review on Amazon

Reviews are not easy to come by, and as an independent author with a little marketing budget, I rely on you, my readers, to leave a short review on Amazon.

Even if it is just a sentence or two!

So if you really enjoyed this book, please...

>> Click here to leave a brief review on Amazon.

I truly appreciate your effort to leave your review, as it truly makes a huge difference.

Chapter 9

Keeping Your Goats Healthy

How To Care For Your Goats

Good and proper care of your goat is one skill you must learn for a successful and thriving goat business. When your goats we healthy, it increases production and your profit. This is why you should take the health of your goats seriously.

The following tips will help you in taking good care of your goats.

Exercise

It's good to allow your goats to exercise. Generally, goats like climbing. Assist them when they need to climb and give them your toys that are related to climbing. Because they enjoy playing, create a space where they can play and run freely.

Deworming

Goats are susceptible to parasites. Therefore, goats must be dewormed frequently. Some of these parasites cause weight loss, reproductive problems and sometimes, death. Therefore, regular deworming is compulsory. The kids should have their first deworming when they are 6 to 8 weeks.

Vaccination

Vaccination should be done at the right timing. It should be done yearly with CDT vaccine. You should vaccinate the kids at 6-8weeks of life and they can take a boost in four weeks. Subsequently, they can be vaccinated yearly.

Bloating

You should avoid giving your goats excessive lush green food because it makes them bloat. Bloating is dangerous and can kill a goat.

Grooming

When your goats are groomed daily, not only will they look beautiful, they will also remain healthy. They should always have a thorough bath and brushing. It's important to trim the hooves at least once a month because it prevents the hooves from bending, cracking and getting infected.

Have a Safe Environment For Your Goats

It's important to create a safe environment for your goats. This will make the goats grow strong and fit, yet excited.

For their safety, you should:

- Have a good fencing facility.
- Ensure that the goats live in a good shelter.
- Provide healthy nutrition and ensure they feed regularly and properly.
- Allow permanent access to clean and fresh water.
- Never feed your goods harmful food.

Conclusion

You read this book because you wanted to acquire knowledge about goats and the process of raising them.

You must keep in mind that if you don't put into practice what you have read in this book, then you will not achieve the results written in each chapter of this book. Don't discard or ignore any information as it has been written.

To kickstart your goat-raising adventure, you must choose the right breed of goats you want to raise, you can always talk to other goat breeders to know more about all the breeds of goat. Get the necessary information about the goats you are buying. Be vigilant when you go goat-shopping, scrutinize the goats, ask as many questions as you should. Don't buy a goat if you have doubts or are not convinced that the goat is good for the price and for the purpose you need them for.

Thereafter, create a system that works on your farm. Make the environment safe, clean, and healthy for the animals. Ensure that your animals are safe from predators. Get enough helping hands on your farm. Get competent personnel that will help you achieve the result that you desire.

Pay attention to their health. They must be vaccinated and dewormed at the right time; you can raise happy, strong, and healthy goats if you consider these measures.

I hope you have the best experience raising your goats.

References

M., Gal, S. L. C., L., Gal, S. L. C., B., J., C., Gal, S. L. C., Crowder, M., Gal, S. L. C., A., Gal, S. L. C., A., L., Gal, S. L. C., M., Gal, S. L. C., S., Gal, S. L. C., Davies, P., . . . Gal, S. L. C. (2019, October 6). *Goat breeds list. Choose the best fit for your family.* Simple Living Country Gal. https://simplelivingcountrygal.com/goat-breeds-list/

Walker, K. (2018, April 3). *How to Buy a Goat*. Gifts from Goats.

https://www.giftsfromgoats.com/home/2018/how-to-buy-a-goat

Lee, A. (2020, November 25). *How to Clean Goat Poop.* Farmhouse Guide. https://farmhouseguide.com/how-to-clean-goat-poop/

S. (2020b, November 16). *Feeding a Goat Requires Knowing What, When, and How Much.* New Heritage Feed Co. https://www.newheritagefeedco.com/feed-a-goat/

Farm, R. (2021, March 1). *Goat Breeding: How to Breed Goats (Guide For Beginners)*. ROYS FARM. https://www.roysfarm.com/goat-breeding/

Wolford, D. (2019, October 7). *How to Disbud & Dehorn a Baby Goat*. Weed 'em & Reap. https://www.weedemandreap.com/how-disbud-dehorn-baby-goat/